If you plan to go into **ANY** home-based business, you'll save time **and** money if you read this book. I tell you FACTS—both good AND bad—so that you might make an *Informed decision* and choose a company and/or business that is best for you.

If you want a **CHANCE** to get rich, or at least a chance to make some extra money working from your home, it's smart to know what you're doing **BEFORE** you begin.

I want you to start a home-based business, but you need to choose one that gives you every chance to succeed. I research products and companies. I'll tell *you* how to do it.

"How can I start a business?" you ask. "*I have a family to feed, I have no money to invest, no bank will make me a loan, and it costs MONEY to start a new business . I don't even have a high school diploma.*

"*Plus, I have no special skills other than what I've done all of my life at a JOB. What kind of business can I go into with all THAT stacked against me? What could I POSSIBLY do?*"

You CAN do it. This book has ALL the answers.

"If you think you can, or think you CAN'T, YOU'RE RIGHT!"

YOUR HOME-BASED BUSINESS

HOW TO MAKE IT WORK
(Over 3.5 million in print)

by

PETE BILLAC

Swan Publishing

Author: Pete Billac
Editor: Mark Mundy
Layout Artist: Sharon Davis
Cover Design: John Gilmore

OTHER BOOKS BY PETE BILLAC:

The Annihilator
The Last Medal of Honor
How Not to Be Lonely—TONIGHT
All About Cruises
New Father's Baby Guide
Willie the Wisp
Managing Stress
Justice Is Green
Natural Air
Shoot for the Stars

Copyright @ January 2007 (Revised edition, 19th printing)
Library of Congress Catalog Card #2003090413
ISBN# 0-943629-54-3
ISBN# 978-0-943629-54-4

YOUR HOME-BASED BUSINESS is available in quantity discounts through: Swan Publishing, Southwind Ranch, 1059 CR 100, Burnet, TX 78611

e-mail: swan@swan-pub.com, www.swan-pub.com
Phone: (512) 756-6800 Fax: (512) 756-0102

Printed in the United States of America.

FOREWORD

This is a "*meat and potatoes*" book in that I tell you LIKE IT IS! I sincerely want you to start a business from your home and SUCCEED! Far too many start these "things" and break even or lose money.

I never promise or guarantee you riches, that's entirely up to you. What I do guarantee is that you have a *chance* to make more money. If you don't try, you *have* no chance.

I ask that you "play" this business like a GAME and have fun doing it. I tell you how to be successful in this business, but like a house, you have to begin with a strong foundation. I absolutely never suggest that you SELL anything; just TELL. You need NOT be a salesperson to succeed.

I research companies and *researchers*. I find PRODUCTS that "make sense." Without a product that "the masses" want or need, your chance of success diminishes greatly. That's one reason so many FAIL in a home-based business; they have a product like everyone else has, or the product doesn't do what the company SAYS it will do.

Yes, read this book and let's see if it "makes sense" you. If it does, give it to a friend.

DEDICATION

To those who want to be their own boss,
and make it happen.

INTRODUCTION

Welcome to a **NO-NONSENSE** guide on going into business for yourself. If you've wanted information on how you can start a home-based business and become successful—it's in this book. You CAN earn $1,000 a month or a MILLION dollars a year.

Can I PROMISE that? **Of course NOT!** I don't know you, your work ethics or your DESIRE to become rich. But I CAN promise that if you don't TRY, or if you don't THINK you can, you won't have a chance to find out. It isn't *easy* to get rich. If it was, EVERYBODY would be rich.

When I talk about earning a MILLION DOLLARS, it scares most people; most can't envision earning a million dollars. But MANY are doing it! I know them! I SAW THEIR CHECKS!

Will YOU earn a million dollars? Maybe. Chances are you won't, the odds are not in your favor. But you'll never know that answer unless you TRY. You've heard that saying; *"If you don't TAKE chance, you'll never HAVE a chance."*

I have MANY stories in this book about people JUST LIKE YOU who wanted more for their family. They found the "right" company, with the "right" product, and I helped them find a "system" that suited *their* personality.

They never SOLD a thing, they started with very little money, NO prior training and no formal education and they were SUCCESSFUL. This book tells HOW they did it and how YOU can do it.

Oh, I guess it's time to tell you about my writing style. I write with words that are CAPITALIZED, *italicized*, **bold faced,** and with "quotation marks." I am *after* only SUBSTANCE and COMMUNICATION.

Since most of my books are in the *How-To* category, I want to make ABSOLUTELY CERTAIN that there is **no room** for even a *hint* of MISINTERPRETATION in what I have to say.

And, YES, I get letters, emails and telephone calls at least a few times each week from avid readers, *pure* writers, English teachers, literary critics and grammarians, ALL chiding me over my writing. NONE have ever written a book. This is my 57th book with 46 selling more than a million copies each.

As a kid in grade school, teachers said I had a fantastic memory, not smart, a good MEMORY. I *remember* a six-line example of how a single word EMPHASIZED changes the meaning of the *entire* sentence: **I NEVER SAID HE STOLE THAT!** Read it and see what I mean.

I never said he stole that!
I **NEVER** said he stole that!
I never **SAID** he stole that!
I never said **HE** stole that!
I never said he **STOLE** that!
I never said he stole **THAT**!

What I'd like you to know is that I *like* helping people make money; it makes ME feel good. And, I don't want ANYONE to have to read a menu from right to left, letting cost dictate your wants.

And, what I want you to know is that there is (probably) NO CHANCE of you **EVER** being rich working for someone else at a JOB. You simply HAVE to work AT **YOUR OWN BUSINESS.** If you want to change your lifestyle for the better, I say TRY it and give yourself a CHANCE.

If you need an extra few hundred dollars a month to "make life easier" why NOT work an additional several hours per week for yourself, part time, from your home at your own business. If you want MORE, work longer hours and learn to work *smart.*

I try to "talk" to you in this book the way I'd talk to my best friend, and I do make "light" of a few things but ONLY to make the book a bit more FUN to read. When it comes to your making money, I am dead serious.

I'm not trying to SELL you anything, just this book, and you already bought it! I became rich working for myself and I certainly couldn't have done it at a JOB, working for someone else. I'll tell you *how* I did it, how **others** have done it and **ARE** doing it, and how **YOU** can do it.

Good luck and God bless,
Pete Billac

"In order to HAVE a chance,
you have to TAKE chance."

TABLE OF CONTENTS

WISHES VS. WANTS

"If you merely WISH for something, you wait and HOPE it happens."

WHEREAS . . .

"If you truly WANT something, you go after it until you GET IT!"

Chapter 1

LET'S GET RIGHT AT IT

PYRAMID SCHEMES

I will do my utmost to make this book NOT read like a *sales manual* or a textbook, but rather an INFORMA-TION GUIDE OF FACTS that will help you begin a home-based business—and SUCCEED.

I ask that you read it with an open mind because I'm not trying to SELL you anything. I research my topics like *Columbo, and* I pull *no punches*. I give you well-researched and documented FACTS!

Before we get too far in this book, I'd like to put "one giant dog to rest" about a **PYRAMID SCHEME!** A *Pyramid Scheme* is what (usually) happens around Christmas, the time everyone needs more money to buy presents.

It's when you get a letter in the mail (often from a well-meaning friend) who asks that you send $100 CASH in a BLANK envelope to a person you've never heard of before. And if you do this, the *next week* YOU will receive 15 or 25 letters in the mail all *loaded with CASH money* for you to keep—tax FREE. Greedy and a bit stupid, huh?

A *new twist* is when they include a letter from AN **ATTORNEY** telling you it's LEGAL. **IT IS NOT!** Get the name and address of that attorney, send his "legal guarantee" to the *American Bar Association, and* you'll be saving MANY from losing their money and stop a true PYRAMID SCHEME.

What makes this **ILLEGAL** is because you do NO work, and sell NOTHING, you just entice your friends to put up money. You see, MANY will get "bumped" in the end, because you're not SELLING a product or a service; it's just people sending money to others.

When it ends (**and it DOES**), the poor saps at the **end** get *zilch*. That is why it's against the law, and THAT is a **Pyramid SCHEME!**

This past Christmas, I got an e-mail that wanted me to send a THOUSAND dollars in a *plain brown envelope* to a P.O. Box in some other state and, within a week or two, I'd get $25,000 back. *"Yeah. Right! I'll do that right away."* Woefully, MANY go for this.

A week later, yet another one asked that I send **TEN thousand dollars** in the mail with a "chance" to get $500,000 back! PLEASE, under **NO circumstance** become a victim of one of these scams. **THESE are Pyramid SCHEMES!**

The TRUTH is, SOME people, the ones at the beginning and near the top (who are NOT *arrested*), DO make a lot of money, but the folks on the bottom lose theirs. PLUS, you **never know** if you're "at the top" or not. It truly IS dumb to try these things, isn't it?

Those who THINK they can make this easy money usually LOSE the hard-earned money they have already made, HOPING to make a *lot* of money FAST. Please, don't YOU become a victim of a pyramid SCHEME! It's not only ILLEGAL, it's downright stupid.

MOST people lose their *entire* investment. Some get their friends involved who lose *their* money, *and* their friendship. And some know it's illegal but greed sets in. They KNOW it's a scam, yet they *still* do it.

And when they lose (and they WILL), they call EVERY home-based business a "Pyramid Scheme." They *deserve* to be one of those **at** the bottom who lose. Yes, please DON'T fall prey to these things, and do NOT tell your friends to try them.

MLM IS A PYRAMID SCHEME

IT IS NOT! This is an **INCORRECT STATEMENT** made by people who just **DON'T KNOW WHAT THEY'RE TALKING ABOUT!** Most *HEARD* about it from someone who failed, or who never understood what they were doing (or didn't work), and/or those who **really** don't know what t*hey* were talking about.

For those who INSIST that a home-based business is a pyramid scheme or a scam without researching it, or those who refuse to listen to common sense reasoning, don't **fight** with them. Hand them this book. It "gently" insults this kind of thinking (several times) and EXPLAINS all they need to know about getting involved in a *legitimate* home-based business.

Yes, hand them this book. In a week or so pick up the book. If they read it and understand it, you have a chance to interest them in *your* business. If they *haven't* read it, you might give then a few more days to read it. If they haven't, take the book back.

If they don't listen to you about your business *after* reading this book, chances are that you are WASTING YOUR TIME! Just PASS THEM UP and pray for them. This is a "numbers" game, and the more people you TALK TO the greater your chances.

Did you get that word, **TALK**? And **GAME**? Yes, just TELL, never SELL. People LOVE to buy, but HATE being SOLD. If, after you talk to them and they refuse to listen, go to the NEXT person. Don't be hurt of offended; **SW, SW, SW? N. (Some WILL, Some WON'T, So WHAT? NEXT.)**

Treat your business like a GAME. Have FUN doing it and make money while having fun. Try not to get "bent out of shape" if they *don't see it the way you see it.* Just make a GAME out of TELLING everyone about what you're doing.

Many call Network Marketing a PYRAMID. It IS a pyramid. EVERY business is a PYRAMID. The BOSS is at the top and his workers work for *him.* Some of these workers work harder and smarter, and they are *under* the boss, but *over* the other workers. The higher you are, the more money you make.

I'M a pyramid; I'm CEO of a publishing company. NONE of my workers make as much as I do. I'm at the TOP of my own *pyramid.* If they want to be at the top of

THEIR own pyramid, they should QUIT and form their own company.

MULTI-LEVEL MARKETING

One of the first Multi-Level Marketing companies was *Shaklee;* they began in 1956. They were followed by *Amway* (the *most* well-known) in 1959. Then came an outpouring of *like* companies including: *Nature's Sunshine, Forever Living, Herbalife, NSA Nutritional's, Mary Kay*, etc., etc., etc. These are NOT Pyramid Schemes; they are *legitimate businesses*.

It's just that SO MANY **DO** FAIL in this type of business because of a myriad of reasons. They lose their investment, they lose their time, it can break their heart and their spirit, and they (usually) alienate their friends, neighbors, and relatives trying to SHOVE "their business" ON them.

The FACTS are, this type of business has made MORE millionaires in the past two decades than all other businesses combined.

**Network Marketing is the EASIEST, the FASTEST,
and the LEAST EXPENSIVE way
there is to go into business for yourself
with a CHANCE to make money while
working from your own home.**

The start-up cost is nominal compared to *any other*

type of business, and there are **new** companies with INNOVATIVE IDEAS starting every day. They designed it where ANYBODY can become successful; you just need to **learn** about it, **understand** it, believe **IN** it, then **DO** it.

PLUS, you do NOT need any formal education or prior training, no STORE (other than your home); you just need the DESIRE to make money by working for *yourself*. The only thing left is for you to ACT on that desire and begin. Plus, there are many TAX advantages in owing your own business.

DREAM STEALERS

I run into this problem ALL THE TIME! Many *"out there"* will warn you NOT to get involved in a home-based business because it won't work. Well, it certainly **won't work for THEM**; they've already convinced themselves of that. If they think it WILL work, or if they think it WON'T—THEY ARE RIGHT!

PLEASE, do not allow them to *dissuade* YOU and hurt YOUR chances of getting ahead. They might *mean* well, but **THEY DO NOT KNOW!** The HARM they (unknowingly) do, is to those who listen to them and never TRY! I call them *"Dream Stealers."*

No matter how well-meaning these folks are, their total **MIS**information and **MIS**conception of Network Marketing as a PYRAMID SCHEME is entirely WRONG! **THEY are wrong! Their ideas of Network**

Marketing are **WRONG!** Hopefully, this book will set them straight and if NOT, don't YOU fall prey to their negative ideas that are totally **UN**founded!

NETWORK MARKETING

I think the *easiest* way to explain Network Marketing is people talking with people, who talk with people, who talk with more people, etc. It's a whole line of people **telling** other people about the product(s) or services they represent. They use personal contact, the telephone, the Internet, direct mail, newspapers, any way they can think of to "get the word out."

There are *networking* businesses in just about every city in the WORLD where people meet and help each other sell or MARKET their wares. It is a **LEGITI-MATE home-based business**, and a way to work for yourself and earn extra money. I'd like to see EVERY-ONE at least TRY it if they want or need more income and/or have a desire to work for themselves.

About eight years ago I wrote the first version of *this* book, but called it **THE MILLIONAIRES ARE COMING.** The book sold well, but **NOT** a best seller. I determined that it was the TITLE that needed revising. In the reprint I changed the title to **THE NEW MILLION-AIRES.** Sales were OK but STILL not what I expected.

I took a long look at the title (again), and determined that MOST people can't *envision* becoming a MILLIONAIRE with just a few hundred bucks invested.

"*I gave them a goal they couldn't see.*" I SCARED them with that "millionaire" title. But many **HAVE** made a million dollars in Network Marketing starting with NOTHING.

It *has* happened to many, it **IS** happening to many, and it will **CONTINUE TO HAPPEN** for those who work it. **I've SEEN THE CHECKS! It COULD happen to you!** I've seen thousands who didn't believe that this was possible, and made any number of excuses *not* to try.

Then, some DID decide to TRY it and to learn about it and then, "*They SAW the big picture*" and went on to have their own successful business. They just had to keep an "open mind" and TRY.

MY PART IN THIS

When I first decided to write about Network Marketing, I just wanted to help people work part-time and make an extra $500 to $1,000 a month. This much, added to most salaries (believe it or not) would change the lives of maybe 95% of the people in the WORLD.

I wanted MOM to be "there" when the kids got home from school. There is NO friend, mother-in-law, aunt, neighbor or babysitter who can "do" with kids the way a parent does.

I wanted DAD to NOT come home from ONE job, *wolf down* food and rush out to ANOTHER job, coming home late and not spending time with his wife or kids. That's no kind of LIFE; that's a SENTENCE.

That kind of life results in stress, arguments, and an **UN**happy *existence*. Marriages dissolve over money problems above all other reasons.

What's wrong with an extra $300, $500 or $1,000 a month working from your home a few hours each week? MILLIONS ARE DOING IT! If you want a chance to make **BIG** money, you work longer hours and you work *smart*. Find a PRODUCT you like and GO FOR IT!

Perhaps YOU don't have the funds or experience to investigate companies, but **I DO**; it's my business. I spend a LOT of time AND money "looking into" various businesses. If I like the PRODUCT, I then find out about the pay plan, investigate the corporate officers and find out about the TRAINING.

WARNING

Do NOT let a friend or relative, or anyone talk you INTO a business or try to SELL you on a business. Most of the time they don't know what they're talking about, or they heard it from a "silk suit" in front of a room full of people who didn't know what THEY were talking about.

Your friend might have all good intentions, but perhaps *they* are desperate or *they* don't have facts, or they were SOLD on it by a pitch that SOUNDED good. GET facts! Ask QUESTIONS!

Far too often a person (friend, relative, neighbor) is talked into one of these businesses and many join just to "get you off their back" and NEVER do anything without constant supervision, pep talks, continued persuading—it does NOT work out.

If YOU are involved in a business that "sounds good," remember that your TIME is important. Spend it with those who "see the picture" the way you see it, and work with them. Do NOT beg, coerce, intimidate or obligate a friend to join you unless you KNOW what you're talking about.

NEVER "go into" a business because you are *desperate* for money. I compare that to someone who is walking; they'll buy ANY car that even "seems" good and they end up with a "lemon." GO into a business ACADEMICALLY. If you LIKE the product, if it makes SENSE to you, if the pay plan is good, LOOK into it some more; this book tells you WHAT to look for. If EVERYTHING "checks out," then **GO FOR IT!**

WHY MLM GOT A BAD NAME

Because **SO MANY FAILED!** Well, that's one reason, but let's talk FACTS! Let's find out WHY they failed. I researched more than 150 of these companies in the past that failed in the 1960's to the 1990's. You'll be surprised WHY.

I think the main reason was that many made a LOT of money with *Shaklee, AmWay, Herbal Life* and a few others—as SALESPEOPLE—and decide to go into business for themselves. Most had NO IDEA how to RUN a business. *"Just because you can FLY an airplane doesn't mean you can BUILD one."*

They went in without sufficient funds (and it costs a LOT of money for start up), they had limited business experience and had no earthly idea what problems lay ahead.

MANY did *too well*. Doesn't make sense that you did so well that you went out of business, but here's how THAT happened.

Computers weren't perfected and they had NO WAY to keep up with taking records. If they got a lot of distributors in quickly, many records were lost or misplaced or the product wasn't delivered or more importantly, MONEY was not paid.

OR, since most of these companies went to some manufacturing facility to get their products, when their sales did so well and so many distributors joined, they had no way of getting product out. You MUST *"get ammunition to your troops."*

Yes! The first month they had 2,000 orders, the next month they had 10,000 orders, and the NEXT month they had **100,000** orders They could NOT "keep up" and the company folded. And when THIS happens, the distributor's tongues begin wagging.

You know the saying: *"When people are happy, they tell their friends and loved ones. But when they are UNHAPPY, they tell EVERYONE THEY MEET."*

Many times, the DISTRIBUTORS THEM-

SELVES were the cause of a company closing down. Far too many distributors MISREPRESENT their product to make it more appealing to a consumer, or **GUARANTEE** a person a sizable income (which is IMPOSSIBLE to do). The *company* is then held responsible for *their* actions and gets closed down.

All Network Marketing companies, *now*, are advised by their attorneys to **NOT ALLOW** their distributors to place an ad, make a statement to the newspapers, conduct radio or television interviews, do their own newsletters, or even go on the Internet unless the COMPANY approves each word.

SOME distributors SAY STUPID THINGS that *could* get the FDA or FTC or any number of these "*watchdog*" agencies against the company. When the COMPANY is closed down, EVERYONE suffers!

NOW, Network Marketing companies set down firm RULES on what a distributor can and can't do. They are CONSTANTLY either warning these rule-breakers, or putting them OUT of the company. Yes, NOW, the rules have changed, but distributors (members) are STILL breaking these rules.

LET'S BARBECUE THE FEDS

It's always fun to "*barbecue* the *Feds*." Contrary to popular opinion, I do *NOT* feel that EVERY person in politics is "*on the take*," power hungry, a drunk, a womanizer or evil. Many TRULY want to help build a better nation, economy, etc. BUT, they are all human and subject to frailties like the rest of us.

A state Attorney General making $60,000 a year after graduating from college and law school, it isn't a lot of money. And not an *easy pill to swallow* to learn of a *retired schoolteacher*, a *garbage truck driver*, or some former *pizza delivery boy* are all making ten, twenty, thirty or FORTY thousand dollars a MONTH in Network Marketing (some working only *part*-time).

This simply HAS to "*rankle the soul*" to learn that all that schooling and hard work nets YOU so little while THEY are making so much. So, *some* public servants (I've seen *them*, too) are much too quick to jump in and try to close the company down.

Sure, it's their JOB to protect the *naive*, but a stern WARNING—maybe followed by a fine to a company—would be a better move in most cases. I don't like laws that HURT the innocent.

Just because *some* of the distributors in a company are *fruit cakes, nut cases* or *liars* should not close down the COMPANY thereby hurting so many innocents. RECENTLY, the "feds" went after the ones who broke the laws and NOT the company. I liked that!

This happened, *often,* a decade or more ago. Now, there are attorneys who specialize in setting up Network Marketing companies and this rarely happens. Yes, NOW it is much safer.

COMPETITION

No matter WHAT you invent, concoct, formulate or discover, SOMEBODY will try to **COPY CAT** it and sell it cheaper, get it out faster, promise a better pay plan, or offer more amenities.

Do you remember the *Health Rider*, that rowing-type exercise machine that you sit on and exercise using your own body weight? A friend of mine, *Lloyd Lambert,* invented it. It sold for about $500. *Covert Bailey*, best-selling author of *Fit or Fat*, was their primary spokesperson. The company made a fortune.

BUT, within **minutes** of the *first* TV campaign, about **five** *other* machines appeared on the market, ALL selling for less. None were as sturdy, or as attractive, but the PRICE was less and this hurt the *Health Rider* sales.

People GO for price. BUT, when you EXPLAIN that there IS a difference, if you KNOW what you're talking about, if you are HONEST with them—if you can get them to LISTEN—you make your sale.

I RESEARCH these companies and get information from those smarter than me. I hire scientists, nutritionists, attorneys and researchers who have NO "hidden agenda." They give me solid information, and once I find out WHAT they're talking about, I put it in words "ordinary humans" can understand without a college degree or a dictionary at their side.

I also have a team of my friends whom I (lovingly) call my *Guinea Pigs*. These people will try ANYTHING as long as it's free. I get THEM to test the product. I test the product, and than I go to the experts who give me scientific answers that I convert to "human" words.

STATISTICS

I'll not bombard you with *statistics*, because those aren't always accurate. It depends on *WHO* does the survey. Besides, I can't be aware of EVERYTHING happening in the rest of the world. My concern is what's going on in MY world—and YOURS! I absolutely NEVER trust statistics.

I remember hearing *statistics* when I was only a ten-year-old. Statistics said, "*America was prosperous and that the average American family was earning $10,000 a year.*"

These "statistics" were from a *long* time ago. My father was a house painter with a fourth grade education earning $35 a week, BEFORE taxes, and I don't want to add or multiply, but that was much less than **$10,000** a year. I guess we were below average.

When the roof leaked from 20 different places in the two-bedroom shack we lived in, and we ran out of pots and pans to catch the water, we had to wait maybe *three paydays* to save the $7.50 for a roll of tar paper (including tar and nails). No, I didn't see **my** world as prosperous.

I'm not soliciting PITY when I tell you this; we didn't KNOW we were poor because EVERYBODY in my area was poor. My father knew ONLY how to paint houses, and they never paid painters very much. I loved and admired him, but as I grew older and a bit smarter, I knew that I never wanted to be poor, and that it was up to only ME to change that.

As a fun-loving 21-year-old, there were more *statistics* that said, *"Ski Aspen! Guys, the women are* **eight deep** *at the bar."* I rushed to Aspen. This was one time statistics were correct; women WERE eight deep at the bar, but MEN were **TWENTY-EIGHT** deep! So much for statistics.

NO GUARANTEE

I use the word "CHANCE" often in this book because, **THERE IS NO GUARANTEE** on a business OR with your job. The biggest **guarantee** is YOU, your desire to make a lot of money, and the sacrifices YOU are willing to make to EARN this money.

Large companies move IN and move OUT smaller ones. Dozens of *Mom and Pop* shops closed that had been there for *generations*. Neighborhood bookstores are fast disappearing because these giant stores that have an inventory of over a MILLION books came in and offered discounts, serve *Starbucks* coffee, and are great social gathering places.

Or, management changes and you might get a

real *jerk* for a new boss. Or you are laid off, or forced into early retirement so they can hire "younger" people and pay them less. Or the owner has a relative to take your job.

I think it's SMART to be IN BUSINESS FOR YOURSELF where *you alone* control your destiny. Network Marketing is NOT "*the wave of the future*," it's here NOW! It's inexpensive to TRY, it's easy to do, and remember—**ANYONE CAN DO IT!**

DO NOT BE DISSUADED

You will ALWAYS have those who STILL believe that Network marketing is a scam, a pyramid, or that *everyone fails in it.* Many do not believe the amount of money you are talking about exists. You, absolutely, MUST pass these people by. You tried to convince them and didn't, but do NOT let THEM convince *YOU* that YOU cannot make it, because YOU CAN! LOAN them this book. If the book can't convince them, trust the fact, YOU can't.

Please, NEVER *lose faith* because others can't "*see what you see.*" Let them remain in their own *financial quagmire* while you surge ahead. You simply MUST believe in YOURSELF. You CAN do it if you make up your mind TO do it. Here's a great "*for instance*" many of you know about.

"In May of 1954 Roger Bannister, a young Oxford medical student, accomplished the impossible; he

broke the 4-minute mile.

"For YEARS, the best runners in the world had failed this quest because most psychologists and sports *brains* said it was PHYSICALLY IMPOSSIBLE for the human body to sustain the stress and physical exertion necessary to run a mile under 4 minutes. Most athletes agreed.

"Bannister refused to believe that he could not do it. He believed that training and DESIRE could conquer the impossible. When the starter's gun fired that day in May, Bannister charged into history flying around the track in 3:59:4. HE HAD BROKEN THE 4-MINUTE MILE! He had ACCOMPLISHED the impossible.

"In the year AFTER Bannister broke the record, SIXTEEN OTHERS ran the mile in less than 4 minutes. Yes, now that the PSYCHOLOGICAL barrier was broken the *impossible* became POSSIBLE."

Whether you make it or not in ANY business is solely dependent on one person—YOU. If you have a self-imposed psychological *barrier*, think about the *Roger Bannister* story.

Years ago I was a professional diver; that underwater *stuff*. One day I got a call that a small plane had crashed in Lake Pontchartrain in New Orleans.

My crew of three and I raced to the crash site. Still in the 4-passenger plane were three passengers, all dead. The pilot was missing.

We searched for the missing body for hours. We returned the next morning at daylight. That evening we discovered the body, approximately two miles from the crash site—**SIX FEET FROM WATER SHALLOW ENOUGH TO STAND IN!**

I had no way of knowing the circumstances. The pilot might have used his very last bit of energy to get to where he was. But, I reasoned, he simply MUST have had enough strength left to make *one more stroke* or *one hard kick.*

My eyes showed tears, and my stomach felt as if a storm was inside. What effort DID he make? Was it despair, exhaustion, or did he just QUIT? That instance help mold my entire life. I NEVER quit!

AN ERROR AND A MYTH

Some people say that Network Marketing companies charge MORE for their product because there is a chain of people UNDER them who must be paid. THIS is simply **not true**. Actually, it's almost a "wash."

A RETAIL outlet has a substantial markup on their products, since they, too, have a long "line" of expenses. The manufacturer makes a profit, getting products delivered, cost for employees, insurance, a building, advertisement, taxes, theft, etc.

A big PLUS is that most NM companies have products that you cannot FIND in retail stores. Also, a distributor knows MORE about their particular product than most store clerks, and what you buy is DELIVERED TO YOUR DOOR.

Chapter 2

INGREDIENTS FOR SUCCESS

THE FIRST INGREDIENT

There are SEVERAL criteria to give yourself the best CHANCE at success, and ALL experts concur that the very FIRST STEP in ANY home-based business is that you find the right **PRODUCT.** You need a PRODUCT that is either . . .

1. UNIQUE, INTERESTING, NEW and/or EXCITING.

2. Something that people WANT or NEED.

3. A product that is BETTER (in some way) than a similar product.

4. If it is THE SAME AS other products, you have to "get" this product to the consumer faster or cheaper than your competition.

5. At the start of/or near the beginning of a TREND

At least twice each week, I am contacted to write a book about a company. I refuse MOST. I must FIRST, *believe in* the PRODUCT. No matter WHO tells you about "*their business*," without a PRODUCT that helps *the masses* in some way, there IS no business!

There are hundreds—actually THOUSANDS— of companies with products that **they** feel are superb and/or unique. There are dealers/distributors/members/ associates of these companies that swear their product will *grow horns on chickens* or any number of other preposterous claims.

If that product is something that has absolute PROOF that it will do what these companies SAY it will do and you can make or save money or live healthier using this product, that's a great start.

The product must also be a consumable or something that people use over and over again; that's how you build residual income.

I list several products that "make sense to me" in a later chapter. I'm (still) not trying to SELL you any- thing, just point you in the right direction. Then, YOU decide which product and company you feel comfort- able in exploring.

When I talk about product, I'm also including a SERVICE. With this modern technology there are all sorts of SERVICES that are terrific for HELPING you market your business.

THE SECOND INGREDIENT

If you like the PRODUCT, go to the second step —MONEY! ASK how MUCH you are going to be **PAID** for marketing these products, and when? Look at the **PAY PLAN** to make certain that it is *"distributor friendly."* That's what you're really working for, isn't it? More money? So, ASK QUESTIONS.

Do not let a friend, neighbor or relative TALK you into anything involving business. Deal with it from "the head" and ask the questions involving the "ingredients" I'm telling you about.

THE THIRD INGREDIENT

The third ingredient involves the corporate officers. I look for several things; *experience*, a winning "track record," and INTEGRITY. If I don't believe and believe IN them, I stop there.

Integrity is the MOST IMPORTANT ingredient for me when I interview and run background checks on these corporate officers. If I feel they are crooks or liars I pass them up.

I look for their past successes in business and a lot about their personal lives. I'm not always right, because I can't find out ALL of it, but I find out MOST of it to satisfy my research and tell YOU about it.

I list *money* as an important ingredient with a company. I LOVE *success stories* where a group meets in a basement and formulate a business that makes millions.

However, if I am to ADVISE OTHERS on a business, I sincerely *prefer* that the people who are starting this business have MONEY in the bank.

I applaud bright entrepreneurs. BUT, as much as I admire those who DO begin their business *"starting on a shoestring,"* far too many end up HANGING THEMSELVES with that same string.

MONEY is important to have when you start ANY business, it helps you *"weather that storm"* of mistakes, new laws, and any number of *"glitches"* that happen that first year or so in ANY business.

THE FOURTH INGREDIENT

TRAINING is an essential part of every successful business. The company you choose MUST have a PLAN OF ACTION—a SYSTEM of some sort—where they get information to their distributors to TRAIN them.

You see, you **CANNOT** *always* count on the one who *sponsored* you into this business to train you. Perhaps they don't really know the business themselves, maybe they are bad teachers, and some get you "in" and then abandon you. LOOK for a distributor that you feel confident KNOWS the business and will train you. YES, ask questions.

I look for the TRAINING PROCEDURES in each company I choose to write about. If the person that sponsored you is a *flake* and won't train you, the COMPANY must see that you are trained. If everything else checks out and the TRAINING doesn't—I pass.

These are the BEGINNING ingredients if you

plan to be successful in your home-based business. Without ALL of these ingredients, your chances of success diminish drastically. There's more.

LEARNING

From here on, it is ALL up to you to LEARN about your products. The first rule of marketing anything is to *"KNOW what you're talking about."*

When you are asked a question, please know the answer. If you DON'T know it, TELL the person that you'll FIND the answer. Be *"up front"* and they will respect and believe in you. FACT!

There are training session, tapes, brochures, catalogs and sales aids in each of these organizations. It's a business—YOUR business—and you MUST learn about it. The more you know, the easier it gets.

DUPLICATION

The ENTIRE THEORY *behind* Network Marketing lies in your ability to **duplicate yourself** in order to get OTHERS working *for* you. In getting down to basics, I'll give you a simple explanation as to how this *duplication* method works, and why it is the **heart and soul** of Network Marketing.

Let's get REALLY BASIC. Take a man who is hired to dig postholes for a large fence company. He is paid $10 a hole. He is earning LINEAR income. We'll cover that definition as we move along.

No matter *how hard* or *how fast* he works it seems that 10 holes per day is his maximum. The most he could ever expect to earn is $100 a day. But the company needed MORE holes dug to sell more fences.

So, this enterprising young man found five of *his* friends who needed a job, and he hired *them* to dig holes for **$9** each. He showed them how to do it; he DUPLICATED himself. He is NOW earning RESIDUAL income.

He still earned his $100 a day digging his own holes, but **also** $10 from each of his five employees who also dug their maximum of 10 holes, or $50 a day extra from *them*. Then they did the same as he.

They each found five people (25 in total) who were digging 10 holes a day for **$8** a hole. NOW, he earned his same $100 from his efforts, PLUS he was taking in $50 from his five workers, and he was NOW getting **another** $1 a hole times 10 holes from 25 workers, or TWO HUNDRED AND FIFTY DOLLARS per day from *their* efforts.

To take it one step further, each of THOSE 25 hired five people each (jobs weren't plentiful then) to dig the same holes for **$7** a day. Want to figure that out? I'll do it for you. He had 125 more hole-diggers earning him an additional $1 per hole times 10 holes or TWELVE HUNDRED AND FIFTY DOLLARS PER DAY! THAT is how "duplicating yourself" earns you big money. THAT is the theory of Network Marketing!

The first hole-digger needn't dig **any more**

holes. His job, then, was to *watch over* the diggers, *cheer them on,* and replace the LAZY ones or those who quit. He was taking in more than FIFTEEN HUNDRED DOLLARS a day! He began working *HARD*, then graduated to working *SMART.* He DUPLICATED his own efforts.

This "*hole-digging example*" is how DUPLICATION works. This is how you get others—*working for you*—**FREE**. Most companies have a variety of compensation plans that don't move down so drastically, and some have dozens of products to replace that single hole.

Let's be sensible, you'll run out of people to DIG those holes, won't you? **NEVER!** You see, you cannot rush down in increments of $1 per hole, sometimes only 10 cents per hole. But, with enough people, those dollars, quarters, dimes, and PENNIES per hole (per hole DIGGER) add up *astronomically.*

Have FUN doing it; make it a GAME.
This way, it really IS easy.
And anyone CAN do it if they truly want to.

YOU WILL NEVER BE INVOLVED IN NETWORK MARKETING

This, of course, is YOUR choice. Everything in life is a choice. Possibly the only things you cannot chose is your parents. After that, it truly IS up to you.

If you do NOT believe (or feel that you can do Network Marketing), **DON'T!** If you do like the product you can always just RETAIL it. The fact is, you'll be leaving a LOT of money "*on the table*." You are looking for RESIDUAL income. If you retail anything, you must keep selling it or the money stops.

In Network Marketing, if you build a *downline*, you'll be paid while you're sick, asleep, on vacation, etc. Oh, there's more to it than that but generally, you truly WANT this *residual* income. I'll explain it as we move along through this book.

EXPONENTIAL GROWTH

I promised not to use any "big" words in this book, but "*exponential*" is easy to explain. Whether you play golf or not is unimportant, just know that there are 18 holes on a regulation course. Let's say someone talks to you about making a wager on a game. You agree to start with betting a PENNY on the first hole, doubling the bet all the way through. Seems safe enough, right? We're talking PENNIES.

The LAST HOLE plays for over THIRTEEN HUNDRED DOLLARS!

Don't believe it? Check it with your calculator. That is the power of GEOMETRIC PROGRESSION, and EXPONENTIAL GROWTH. THIS is how Network

Marketing works. THIS is how YOU can become rich *if* you work hard *and* smart and if you duplicate your own efforts by training others.

That's what I'm going to share with you in this book. It could make you wealthy or, at the very least, change your lifestyle to where you never have to read that menu *from right to left* ever again.

Here is an example of duplication and this "*exponential growth*" I talk about in Network Marketing. A friend of mine had been involved in Network Marketing for a few decades and was living "comfortably" on $75,000 to $80,000 a year.

His JOB netted him about $50,000, and he made $25,000 or so from "playing in" his Network Marketing businesses working part-time. FINALLY, he found a business on the internet that he liked.

I did one FREE radio show for him. Anyone who called in the next 24 hours would get a FREE book. He got 121 calls. After "qualifying them" as I instructed, he agreed to send out 83 books.

Of these, he "signed up" 38 people; 31 quit within a few months. BUT, he trained the 7 who stuck with the business to duplicate his own efforts.

In ONE year, from these SEVEN people who "worked the business," he had over ONE MILLION people from countries all over the world in his *downline*. He became a MILLIONAIRE!

He received WEEKLY checks (for months) of $76,000! I SAW THE CHECKS! He said, "That a few weeks he received checks of $125,000 and more." I didn't see those, but I believe him. He became rich, and traveled the world having FUN!

THAT, my friends, is the power of Network Marketing through DUPLICATION, GEOMETRIC PROGRESSION, and EXPONENTIAL GROWTH!

You WILL meet people **who, for WHATEVER reason, will NOT** "*work the business*" because they don't want to *Network Market* ANYTHING! **Fine!** They can do **DIRECT MARKETING** that I mentioned a page or two earlier. Remember, too, it's not WHAT you do but HOW you do it.

MAKE WORK FUN

It must be absolutely awful to work for money alone, and *have to* make this money. I can think of but a few things worse than not LIKING the work you do.

With Network Marketing, I'll teach you how to make a GAME of it, how to have FUN doing it; enjoy your work. Also, how to NEVER anger your relatives, friends or neighbors or anyone running from you as if you had Yellow Fever.

I'll tell you how to "get involved" in a business that *you* choose, that you can *like*, and that you can help yourself while helping others.

If you STILL don't like Network Marketing, find a product and company that you like and RETAIL their product ONLY. Yes, BUY the product wholesale and sell it retail. But remember, when YOU stop selling, the MONEY stops coming in. You'll enjoy this business (any) business if you treat it like a game.

My insurance man drove 270 miles from Houston to my ranch here in Burnet, Texas. He got out of his car with a huge smile on his face.

"Hi David, good to see you. That big smile must mean that you had a very productive day."

"Actually Pete," he told me. *" I had a terrible day. Two policyholders cancelled, another had an insufficient check, two others switched providers, two others didn't show up for an appointment, one slammed the door in my face, and another's husband threw me out of their house."*

"Then why the big smile?" I asked. *"Statistics say that one out of ten people will buy a large policy, and you are the TENTH person I am seeing today."*

The story was *so good* that I increased my life insurance by $500,000. You see, David made a GAME of it. He knew he had a great product and he persevered. He didn't get "bent out of shape" with those first nine disappointing tries. His attitude was positive.

"Attitude determines ALTITUDE."

Much of what I'm telling you, many of you already know; *knowing* and *doing* are quite different. But then, you know that too. I can promise you this; that there is no better "attitude builder" than being successful in your business and providing a better life for yourself and your family.

"If you WANT something you have never had,
you must be willing to DO something
you have never done."

I don't mean to *bombard* you with these"cliches." it's just that they are ALL so very, VERY true. This is a NUMBERS game and a PEOPLE business.

You develop a system of TELLING others about your business, then, SHUT UP and wait for them to ask questions. If they don't ask questions, TELL a bit more and SHUT UP AGAIN.

If they STILL don't ask any questions, PASS THEM UP! They are either NOT interested, or YOU tell rotten stories. Yes, pass them up, don't be rude, just smile, remain friends and pray for them. Then, go *tell* someone else.

If you learn to tell a good story, people will listen. If you tell a *lot* of people, your chances are great that you'll make a *lot* of money.

NOW, let's talk about your J.O.B. (**J**ust **O**ver **B**roke).

Chapter 3

A JOB

I'm not trying to CONVINCE you of *anything,* and I'm not "knocking" those of you who have a JOB; most of THE WORLD works for somebody else. It's just a proven fact that MOST people will NEVER become financially independent working at a **J-O-B!** As I stated in the introduction, when you work a JOB you help the BOSS get rich—or *richer.*

The main PROBLEM with most **JOBS** is that after you retire, **you STILL have to work.** If you haven't *saved* a sufficient amount of money or invested wisely, your lifestyle will take a serious *dip.* I've SEEN it. My dad, a house painter for 45 years, had to find another JOB the very *day* he retired.

I walk though these big supermarkets, and see many who *appear* to be very old STILL working. *Wal*Mart*, for instance, hire hundreds of thousands of *retirees,* most who NEED that paycheck to live with any degree of dignity.

About 90% of the retired world, AFTER they retire from their J-O-B, are dependent upon RFC: RELATIVES, FRIENDS, and CHARITY!

JOBS I'VE HAD

I feel that many of you can *identify* with these jobs and laugh along with me. I can laugh too—NOW! *Then*, it wasn't a bit funny. We ALL go through these phases in our lifetime. Even many of the movie stars and high paid athletes, went through these "*learning experiences*" on their way to earning big money. FEW start "*at the top*."

One of the very WORST jobs I recall was when I was 11 years old. I was hired to cut the high weeds on some miserable old lady's one-acre lot. My pay was to be six dollars.

The weeds were high, and when I agreed to cut them I had *no way* of knowing that *inside* the first *row* of high weeds were about **500 RAILROAD** TIES that had to be moved and stacked BEFORE I could cut the weeds. I also agreed to MOW it (hand mower in those days—no motor).

I worked 10-11 hours a day for FOUR days. I remember straining, and actually *shoving* those things with my feet to get them out of the way, then straining and spitting as I lifted one end at a time to STACK them! Each one got heavier than the last, and that Louisiana sun was merciless.

The lady brought me iced tea—14 glasses. **SHE KEPT COUNT!** I got my six dollars for the work MINUS 42 cents because she CHARGED me three cents per glass for the tea! I *never* forgot *that* lesson. Ever since then, I do RESEARCH, and ASK QUESTIONS **before** I make a major decision. YOU, please, do the same.

During high school, my "fun summers" were spent in the hot sun but, but *not* on a beach. I worked on a road crew building a highway through the swamps of Louisiana. There were giant mosquitoes big enough to almost carry you off, water moccasins, an occasional alligator, and stifling heat as constant companions.

During my college summers, I did "floor" and "tower" work as a *Roughneck* on offshore oil-drilling rigs. One summer, I chipped paint from a *rust bucket* cargo ship bound for Africa. When we got there, I was *half* done, and the other half I did on the trip back. My arm swung by itself for months.

After graduation, I taught school for a year, married, and had a baby daughter. To supplement my teacher's income, I worked as a longshoreman on the Mississippi River in New Orleans at night.

I got off school at three, made it home, wolfed down food, changed to "work" clothes, was at work by five and worked until 1am, bathed, slept five hours, and did it all again. Anyone reading this will understand what I'm saying? Maybe not the same job, but you've "*been there*" too, haven't you?

These, of course, are "*learning experiences*" we ALL go though. I know that many of you reading this can relate to these JOBS "we held" before settling for what we have. The BIG problem is that far too many are STILL working for peanuts. NOW is the time to try working SMART.

YOUR FUTURE

Let's say you have a job now—*one that you like*—but you're not making what you feel you deserve. You certainly can't QUIT that job; how would you be able to take care of yourself or your family? I say: **START A HOME-BASED BUSINESS ON A PART-TIME BASIS**. It doesn't cost much to TRY, and it truly COULD make life easier for you.

     I told you earlier on in this book that I began my "mission" by trying to help the "*little people*," those who wanted to make an additional $500 or more per month working part-time from their home and who had little money to TRY. USUALLY, when those who do make a few hundred in this business realize that if they put in a little *more* time and effort, they can make *more* money. SEE THE PICTURE?

     WHEN you are taking in **three times** what your regular job is paying for **six months in a row**, THEN quit that regular JOB and work your business FULL-TIME. If you LIKE your regular job, stick with it. How very NICE it is to be able to make a choice.

     And, PLEASE, when you DO start making "big" money, don't "go wild" and buy everything you see. SAVE some of that money in the event something happens to the business. Even though it's YOUR business, you are STILL dependent upon the company to stay in business.

     The GOOD part about this MLM business is that

ONCE YOUR KNOW WHAT YOU'RE DOING, you can become successful with ANY company.

LINEAR INCOME

I've "touched on" the two types of income several pages back, but HERE is what they are. A salary by working a **JOB** is called LINEAR income; you only make more if you work faster or put in more hours. When YOU stop working, the money stops! Most of the **NON-rich** people in the WORLD are earning **LINEAR INCOME.**

My dad earned linear income his entire life. Whatever he made, he spent on food, clothing and shelter. With a fourth-grade education, he knew little about investing, and as far as SAVING, there was NO MONEY *left* to save. THAT is why he had to find another JOB, the *day* he retired as a house painter.

CEO's and heads of giant corporations, the ones who make the BIG money, are at the top of that "*pyramid*" we talked about earlier. YOU are working for THEM, and THEY are paid on YOUR efforts. If they stay home sick, they STILL make money because YOU are working.

But, once YOUR "sick leave" days are used up, when YOU get sick again, your money stops. How can YOU get out of this "linear income" *trap,* and make money even when YOU, personally, DON'T work? How NICE it is to be able to make money when you AREN'T working. If you work SMART, this can happen. I'll tell you how. The short answer is to earn . . .

RESIDUAL INCOME

THESE are two **great words** coupled together; it is **SMART** income. In Network Marketing, you earn "residual" income; you make money even when you DON'T work. Oh, you work at first, but instead or working HARD, you begin working SMART. Doesn't this make sense?

The "work" you do is to train OTHERS to do as you have done, and you build, and build, and BUILD. Then, THEY do as you've done, and you get that RESIDUAL income, the way MOST of the rich people in the world *became* rich.

SOME have made a lot of money in Network Marketing by finding a product they were able to RETAIL, and that's fine. BUT, it's almost the same as a JOB with "linear" income.

When YOU stop retailing, when YOU stop putting in the hours and the effort, your income comes to a screeching halt! I suggest you do BOTH; sell AND recruit. THEN, train the ones you recruit. Duplicate yourself. Get paid while you are sleeping, or resting, or just want to a week or two—or a MONTH or two—off.

The word NETWORK means you tell others about whatever it is you're selling. MARKETING means that you have found ways to MOVE your product! What

SMARTER way is there than to get other "hole diggers" to help, and you PAY THEM NOTHING? And they, of course, can do the same.

When you *teach them* to "dig those holes," you duplicate your own efforts. You are working SMART, and you are producing **RESIDUAL** income. YOU make money, and as *they* get more diggers to help them, then THEY are *also* receiving *residual* income (income that goes on, and on, and on).

If I went bust tomorrow morning, by **noon** I would be in a Network Marketing company. *Donald Trump* said the same thing on the David Letterman show several years ago.

I *NETWORK MARKETED* myself and my books. I have books in thousands of bookstores across America and around the world. When I sleep, or I go on vacation, or when I take off a few days, I am STILL making money. THIS is residual income.

I *duplicated* my efforts though my own *downline* of bookstores, and through the people who work IN these stores. Every time *they* sell a book, the store makes money, they keep their JOB and make money, and I make money. Several of my books are in a dozen or more languages and sold all over the world.

I still work because I LOVE it! Money isn't important, but it's a great way of keeping "count" of how well you do.

MOSTLY I work to help others—no *goody-goody* stuff—I just LIKE it and realize that MY life could have been easier had I gotten help. I ONLY help those who are willing to learn, and willing to WORK.

If you are in this last category, I'll help. If not, please don't waste my time. I have others to help who want to learn, who will put forth effort, and who RE-ALLY want financial success.

WIN AT NETWORK MARKETING

Truthfully, it's like choosing a spouse; 50% fail the FIRST time, another 50% fail the SECOND time, but from experience, if you learn to choose *academically,* your odds of success increase. If you're smart and follow what is written in this book, you MIGHT get it right the FIRST time.

If YOU are willing to make some **changes,** some **concessions**, to **sacrifice** some of your free time, you'll *have* that chance. PLAY with it if you choose, but if you are not **100% committed** to *whatever* you're doing, chances are it won't work in such a way that you'll earn BIG money. If you need help working this business, GET help from your spouse or close friend. Work as a TEAM.

I, personally, am not PERFECT at most things. The percentage that I lack, I have a PARTNER to cover my weak points. It's like a relay race with four runners; if three of those runners are fast and one is a *clog,* you will NEVER win the race.

MOST of the success stories in any and ALL Network Marketing companies is when the husband

and wife work *together*, or you form a "partnership" with someone you like who will ALSO work.

BEFORE you begin, here are some guidelines to follow to become successful in this business. Let's take them one at a time, and if YOU don't have them all, find that partner—that back-up person you can count on—and work together.

❑ **BELIEF IN YOURSELF is first. Then, have belief in your products, your company, and Network Marketing.**

❑ **COMMITMENT: Do *whatever it takes* to get the job done.**

❑ **SET YOUR GOALS: Write them down, and read them *daily*. Dream, and dream BIG! Know the REASONS you want to *achieve* these goals, WHEN you want to achieve these goals, and HOW you plan to do it. Be specific! Frequently REVIEW these goals.**

❑ **DUPLICATION: This is a word that cannot be overused in Network Marketing. It is impossible to succeed alone. Success comes in abundance when you learn the art of duplication. You must BUILD a system that is easily *duplicatable*. Never do anything other people can't COPY! Have a simple plan, one that everyone can follow, and repeat that plan (that system) over and over and over.**

❑   MAKE A LIST: Have someone you just sponsored list 20 of the *most important* people in their life, never prejudging anyone. (YOU do the same when you first start.) From that list of 20 names, select the top five prospects and set an appointment with each for a *two-on-one* presentation or a *three-way* call.

For the presentation, have your *upline* (or mentor) conduct it while you observe and learn. These beginning few prospects are the KEYS to your business. If it's a three-way call, the *upline* still makes the presentation to the prospect and you just listen.

Two things are happening here. First, the *upline* will be *more successful* with the prospect because they *know* the system. Second, *you* are being *trained*. Learn this procedure, and repeat it until you feel confident enough to conduct a presentation yourself.

Invite the remaining people to an in-home presentation where the *upline* looks for the prospects who have *fire in their eyes*, those who recognize the opportunity before them. These potential prospects become the new recruits, and the process starts over again with the former new distributor being the mentor/presenter. This is DUPLICATION!

AFTER you finish with the original 20-people, create an *Organic Prospect List* of maybe 200 (neighbors, friends, relatives, acquaintances across the country or anywhere in the world).

Each week, select *ten names* from the list and make these your *contact people* for the week.

Every week add *five names* to the list, people you meet just walking through life. And remember, NEVER prejudge. You never know who will or who won't be your next leader. If you have but ten new distributors using the same system, after ten weeks you, personally, would have contacted 100 people and if the distributors you trained were trained well, they will have contacted a THOUSAND people! THIS IS DUPLICATION! This is the BIG SECRET of what makes Network Marketing work! PLAN your work, and WORK your plan!

❑ A FOLLOW-UP SYSTEM: Develop a *follow-up system* for your new distributors and for your retail customers. Send them a tape, a BOOK, any piece of literature for a period of time on a regular basis. You MUST follow up!

This introduces *them* to the entire product *line* a product at a time or to the business itself. It is a very effective *drip system* that leads to building great business relationships. It's "the" way to make money.

❑ A SUPPORT TEAM: Have FUN with this business. Treat it like a GAME. Everyone needs a friend, a cheerleader, a *confidante* in the business. When you are UP, it's great to be recognized, and when you're DOWN you'll welcome support. Develop a team of four or five people and create a Support Team.

❏   TEAMWORK: *Everyone working together* will accomplish more. Become a leader in your business; LEADERS make the BIG money. Remember, you are working WITH your distributors, not FOR them. Everyone is in business FOR themselves but not BY themselves. Understanding that each person has different talents allows your distributors to use *their* talents. If you find a leader, *let them lead!*

❏   FOCUS: It's like MAGIC, and gives you a chance for great success in everything you do *especially* in Network Marketing. Focus on ONE company. Rarely can you work two or more successfully. There ARE exceptions, of course. If you want to build confidence in your distributors, the best way to destroy it is to become the mayor, sheriff, fire chief, and postmaster.

❏   VISION: This is the initial step to take in creating the business to which you aspire. Tell your distributors, *"If you could only see what I see."* Remember Helen Keller? She said, *"The most pathetic person in the world is someone who has sight but no vision."*

CAN I MAKE A MILLION?

PROBABLY NOT! Most won't! The "odds" are *not* in your favor. Besides, I don't know you, your abilities, your commitment, or anything about you. Even if I did, as I said earlier, only YOU can guarantee that. All I do is tell you that there is a CHANCE.

BUT, a MILLION DOLLARS is NOT out of reach; MANY are making this much. And a million bucks, even in these days and times, is STILL a lot of money, and is NOT unattainable. But, you can hardly expect to make a million dollars working at a J-O-B.

In the past, earning a million dollars was only for the *Rockefeller's,* the *Ford's*, the *Whitney's,* and the *Vanderbilt's*—movie stars, athletes, the RICH people we only read about. But look around at all the BIG houses, and the people driving those luxury cars; almost ALL are in business for themselves! FEW made this much working at a JOB.

HOW MUCH CAN I MAKE?

Only an educated guess: What **I AM** telling you is if you have the *right* product, with the *right* company and with the *right* pay plan, if you put in 10-15 hours a week, in most instances you can expect $500 or more per month (maybe $1,000) after just a few months. If you want to make more, put in more hours.

This is not a "get rich quick" scheme of any sort; this is a BUSINESS—your OWN home-based BUSI-NESS. With MOST of companies, it will take 12, 15, 18 months before MOST people make any *serious* money. I've watched and researched this business for a LONG time, and I KNOW what I'm saying.

There is ALWAYS a handful of distributors in most of these companies who make over a million or more dollars per year. Those who ARE earning this big money (I've SEEN IT) were either IN some other Network Marketing company in the past where they KNEW what they were doing and had a host of followers, or they worked hard AND smart FULL-TIME!

Figures change, but in the SOLID Network Marketing companies, usually only a handful become millionaires, 1% or so earn in the mid six figures ($300,000 to $600,000 per year) and maybe 2% to 5% more earn just above or around $100,000 in a year. Not bad for a few years effort.

About 10% make $500 to $1,000 a week. These are the ones who work hard but not SMART. The ones who are at or near $1,000 a month are usually *part-timers* who get a few others in their business but don't REALLY work with them. They "might" make a call or two, attend a few meetings, and if their distributors drop out (from lack of direction and attention) they, the *part-timers,* might look for another person to sponsor if they "happen" along.

These are the ones who are not REALLY money-motivated, might have other income from retirement or savings, and sort of "play with" the business. They don't need or want much and they are satisfied with themselves. About 80-85% make expenses, nothing, or *lose money*. These are FACTS!

WHEN TO START

NOW, if you understand and believe in yourself, in the concept, if you find a product you like, and if you have desire. If you are determined that you will ACT upon your desire to make more money by working from your home, you have a great CHANCE to make it all happen. It's up to you!

It makes me smile when people talk about; "G*et in the company early,*" or "*get in on the ground floor,*" or *this is a "ground floor opportunity.*" The truth is: it is often smarter to get into most companies AFTER the first year since so many never make it through that 12-month test!

You see, during the first year in most companies there will always be changes, laws you never heard of, and problems; it's impossible *not* to have them. From the *corporate* standpoint, there will be people to hire, people to fire, people to promote, new methods of communication, new products, and maybe a change in the marketing plan.

If it's a new company, look at what I ask that you do in order to "*qualify*" them. Then, look in the mirror and qualify yourself. Now, sit down and **WRITE your goals**, what you will be willing to sacrifice, and what you will be willing to do.

If it's a company that's been in business for years, you are STILL "*on the ground floor,*" because there is NO AMOUNT of advertising where EVERY-BODY knows about your particular product, regardless of how unique it is. So "*ground floor*" or "*getting in at the beginning*" is a bunch of baloney.

There are about 300 MILLION people in the U.S. alone (census takers never get everyone) and most of them never *heard* of your product. When YOU have made up your mind to TRY Network Marketing, NOW is the time to get involved. THINK about it, and it could pass you by. ACT on that desire and it could make you rich.

START PART-TIME

If you're *new* to this business, **BE CAUTIOUS! Start PART TIME!** Make a CHOICE on a product, and spend as little money as possible until you KNOW WHAT YOU'RE DOING and whether you CAN do it. Sort of "feel" your way.

If you don't WORK the business and fail, don't moan and groan and blame the company; YOU made the choice. If you quit, or jump to another company and you want someone to blame, LOOK IN THE MIRROR and point your finger.

START FULL-TIME

I spoke at a convention in Bournemouth, England a few years ago, and met two guys who *started* FULL-TIME. These guys (Rick and Ray) had been IN Network Marketing for a dozen or more years, and they earned a good living. But, they had never REALLY found the company they liked, with great products and a good pay plan. But when they did, they *went for it.*

They are both multi-millionaires, and they made it in less than two years (THIS time). They persevered! They understood the business, but their (past) products were faulty. Yes, product is first; don't ever think it isn't.

And please don't be *frightened* by "big" money . I have seen people from all walks of life come into this business and make it big. When they do, you'd never guess that many of them were like you—and me—like your neighbor or friend, then suddenly their lives changed forever.

I feel "good all over" when someone calls from the past and thanks me for helping them in their business. We ALL like appreciation, don't we?

Compliment your wife on a good dinner or on how terrific she looks. And compliment your husband on *whatever* he does that is good. Yeah, EVERYONE likes to be appreciated.

This book should help you, and I will help you, but it all comes down to YOU. On, your *desire* to make money, on your *commitment ,* and on your effort. Say this to yourself over and over . . .

"If it is to BE, It is up to ME!"

Chapter 4

WHY PEOPLE FAIL

There are many reasons why people fail in Network Marketing. *Candidly*, I point out that most people who fail at any business is because they were greedy, lazy, or naive (nice word for stupid).

I find that the majority of **UN**successful people didn't have the *desire* to put forth the *effort* to make big money, nor do they act on that desire. Many are happy *"where they are"* and if so, I am happy for you. But this book is about money, and I'm assuming that you're reading it because you'd like to—or need to—make more money.

Many fail because they cannot handle rejection. This is the big one! You get in a business, you learn about it, you believe in it, and when you go out to tell someone about it, and if they *"don't see it as you see,"* you become devastated. Not everyone *will* see it the way you do, and as a result, many become discouraged and quit. Smile and go to the next person.

You can overcome objections by study, by learning the answers, by learning to *counter* rejection. *Then*, rejection becomes a challenge, even fun. Have FUN while you make money.

Another reason many fail (or do not even TRY) is that they are not "suited" to sell things; they are NOT salespeople, and if they are selling (or marketing something), they need to be extroverts and/or sales-minded. **NOT SO!** I have some answers where you need only TELL—never SELL. People love to *buy,* but hate being sold! .

Yet another reason people fail is that they either quit before giving it time, or "jump" to another company. In every Network Marketing company, there are those who do not do well right away, and go over to *another company* hoping to do better. Most don't do better, and blame "the business"!

YOU FAILED BEFORE

So what? *Everybody* fails at some things at some time or another. Abraham Lincoln failed many time before becoming president of the United States.

Let's begin with those of you who were in Network Marketing two or three times (or more) and failed. Let's try to find out *which* of the following errors you made. Just try not to make them again.

❖ **You listened to a friend who meant well, but didn't really know WHAT they were talking about.**

Don't join just to join, or *"to get your friend off your back."* Approach it as a business. Listen carefully. Ask questions, and understand the answers.

❖ **You tried to market the wrong PRODUCT.**

Remember, the product is the FIRST ingredient to success. Without a good product, your chances of success diminish. The MASSES have to want or need the product.

❖   **You QUIT too soon.**
It takes TIME to build ANY business. Even though this business is FASTER THAN MOST, it doesn't happen in weeks or even months. The "average" Network Marketer contacts FEWER than THREE people. How can you be successful in marketing ANYTHING with this effort?

❖   **You were lazy.**
Self explanatory. It IS funny that, almost ALL of the time, the one who WORKS the most (and the smartest) makes the most money. You have to study and LEARN, and give UP some of your "non-cash-producing" luxuries if you want to become rich. THEN, vacation for life.

❖   **You were in too much of a hurry.**
It DOES take time. If you are trying to build a BUSINESS, it takes 12-18 months BEFORE (most) bring in truly BIG money. FEW are immediately successful. It takes TIME for this "exponential growth" to come into play.

❖   **You wanted to work YOUR OWN system.**
I know people who have been **UN**SUCCESSFUL in SEVERAL businesses, but they CONTINUE doing the **SAME THING** and try nothing new. Or, they want

to **RE-WRITE the system** the company has. TIMES change, and if you don't change **with the times**, you are left behind.

❖   **You JUMPED to a better deal.**
     "If you fail in Tulsa, chances are you'll fail in Paris." You need TIME for this truly **marvelous concept** of Network Marketing to work. EVERYONE has a "better mousetrap." Look for the right product and a company you have researched to your satisfaction BEFORE you get involved, and *stick with* IT.

LOOK at these above reasons for failure, and see which category(s) fits you. YOU decide. Did you notice that EACH reason started with **Y-O-U?** In EACH INSTANCE, the failure was with **the person**.

WHAT DO I DO NOW?

You mean once you quit or failed? The toughest part is having to tell your SPOUSE that you failed, but that you'd like to try it *again*! I see it EVERY DAY with people who have to "sneak" around their wives (or husbands) to work a business because they failed before, but their spouse doesn't want them to try it again. Another reason to choose carefully.
     If the spouse *does* (grudgingly) agree, it goes something like this: *"Go ahead and work it, but I want no part of it."* Many threaten a DIVORCE if their spouse tries it **ONE MORE TIME**, or they let them work it

alone! A better CHANCE for success is when **both work together**—in ANYTHING!

The very SECOND I failed, I GOT BACK UP! Did I feel bad? Sure. Did I doubt my own ability? NEVER. I simply WENT TO WORK! And THIS time I was determined to work SMART as well as hard.

Being poor is no fun, but being rich then BE-COMING poor is *devastating.* The poor don't usually know what they're missing, but once you're "*up there*" and get knocked down, *down* comes your dignity, self-respect, desire—and, you lose friends. When I failed, I had two strong motivating factors to get back UP: HUNGER and DIGNITY (in that order).

> *"It's not how many times you get knocked DOWN,*
> *it's how many times you get back UP."*

WHY DID I FAIL?

Answer THAT one yourself. Were you greedy? Naive? Stupid? In a hurry? NEEDED money badly. Most of the time, it starts like this. You needed to make **more money.** Then, some friend invites you to a meeting. The speaker at the meeting tells you how EASY it is to earn $10,000 or $50,000 a month (or more) in *this* company selling *this* product, and that you can do it working a few hours per week.

WOW! This sounds great. *"I can work three hours a week and get rich,"* you tell yourself. Yes! Greedy, naive, AND stupid. The fact is, this HAS happened—but rarely! **DON'T COUNT ON IT!** Get **OUT** of there. They are **LYING** to you.

You need a **PRODUCT**, a **PAY PLAN**, and a **COMPANY** that **YOU BELIEVE IN!** Please USE what I advise in this book. It's about two HUNDRED years of combined study, trial-and-error, and it WILL increase your odds of being successful in this truly FASCINAT-ING business.

MOST PEOPLE FAIL

I was doing a radio show promoting one of the first editions of this book when the host, who was negative on Network Marketing, said:

"Mr. Billac, you SAY you tell the truth in your books. Then, would you agree, that 85% of the people who have been involved IN Network Marketing fail?"

"Yes, that's true, I answered. But then, 85% of the people fail in ANY business. Actually, 95% of the people FAIL IN LIFE!"

HOW CAN I DO IT RIGHT?

MOST Network Marketers alienate their friends, neighbors and relatives by using the WRONG ap-proach. They "corner" these people and try to SHOVE their products or their business down their throat. They bother, badger, intimidate, and even *hunt down* these folks, and NEVER seem to know when it's hopeless. They are trying to "*teach a pig to sing. All they are doing is wasting their own time and aggravating the pig.*"

Just because THEY believe in what they're doing, they expect EVERYONE to "*see the picture*" as *they* see it. They soon get the same reputation as the telemarketer who calls during dinner, or near the end of a television show you've been watching for almost two hours.

I KNOW you've all heard of the "*three-foot rule.*" This is when anyone who comes within THREE FEET of you, you tell them about your products and/or your business. Personally, I can't do this, and if it's done to me, it *turns me off* completely.

I'd rather fight five bikers in a back alley than go up to a *stranger* and begin yapping about what I can do for them. If one of these *three-foot-rulers* comes up to me on a bad day, as sweet and tolerant as I am, they had better be a LOT bigger or I'll slug 'em.

HOWEVER, the ones who have the guts and the personality to do this are usually the **leaders** in companies and make an AWFUL lot of money. They are the ones who say, "*Throw enough spaghetti at the ceiling and SOME of it will stick on.*" They play the "numbers" game. They *understand the business* and they WORK it.

There are METHODS to use where you NEVER have to have ANYONE hiding when they see you. Remember? NEVER sell—TELL! If your product is "good" and you are enthusiastic in TELLING about it, they listen.

If you *believe in* your product, if *you like this business ,* and (hopefully) you know what you're talking about, if what you have makes them feel better, look better, have fun and/or can make them money, you win this "game." If they don't listen or agree, PASS THEM UP and go TELL someone else.

LEARN to TELL a good story, be positive, enthusiastic and NEVER appear desperate. TALK to them as you would a friend, and TELL them how YOU will **HELP THEM** with the business. Show CARE.

"People don't CARE what you KNOW, until they KNOW that you care."

And DO care! It's not only the *RIGHT* attitude; it's also very smart business. **MY WAY** is to tell a *little about* the business, TELL them you recently read a "great" book, try to get them interested in *"the book,"* and loan THIS book to them for a week or so to read.

TRUST THE FACT, they will believe "the book" more than they will believe YOU! I don't know WHY that is but it's fact. Let "the book" do the SELLING for you.

THIS approach allows **NON**-salespeople to feel that THEY can DO the business. They only need to learn about their product, try to understand "the business," then merely "mention" this to others. They need never actually *sell* anything; Tell a little about the business and let the book do the *selling.* It will.

This approach has worked for tens of thousands of people in almost any business I've recommended. Sure! It's my business selling books, but it also works.

FIND A SYSTEM

Listen to your leaders. I do not want to "hear" how to lose weight from a fat person, or how to get rich from a poor person; It doesn't make sense. I believe that, "*If you walk the walk, you can talk the talk*". Your leaders have earned the right to "*talk the talk.*"

Try to do it their way. If you cannot do *exactly* as they say, TELL THEM, and ask them to help find or devise a system that best suits your personality. Then, practice it over and over until you are really good at it. Then teach others, and they in turn will chose their own system that suits *their* personality.

Some of these folks who have become millionaires learned the business, were *enthusiastic* about it, liked doing it, and they worked at it ALL the time.

They worked smart, and they adopted a "system" that suited *their* personality. I say LISTEN to them and *try* it their way.

If you simply *cannot* do it the way they advise, then find a way that does suit your personality, discuss it with them, practice it over and over until you become proficient, then DO it! Use your system on everyone you meet.

I say to treat it as you would a game, and have fun doing it. Try loaning them this book, give them a week to read it. If they haven't read it in, say a week or so, you can either give them a few more days to read it or get the book back and try it on someone else.

You need very *few* people who *"see the picture"* as you do. Get one "good" person a week, teach them, train them, help them, and in a few months you could be earning more money than you've ever imagined possible.

Remember (again); *"People LOVE to buy but HATE being SOLD!"* Never try to sell! Never be a pest! *Tell* your story, and wait for them to ask questions. When they do (most will), your chances of getting them involved in your business multiplies dramatically.

By telling a story, or loaning them this book, they will ask you questions. Do you understand what I'm saying? Now *they* are asking, and all you need do is answer their questions. You are NOT *selling.*

If they do show some interest, direct them to your web site and/or tell them about a meeting or a conference call. Never push. Never look desperate. Never sell. Smile, be confident, and answer their questions truthfully.

MEETINGS ARE NOT GOOD

What I mean is BAD meetings are not good; only GOOD meetings are good. Meetings are the lifeblood of most Network Marketing companies. I love meetings. You meet people, you laugh, and you learn.

I like meetings where the speaker knows their product. I want the speaker to smile, be friendly, and establish some *rapport* with the audience for maybe 10 minutes *before* they begin to talk about the product or the business. This gives those who (always) arrive late, time to get there.

I'd like the main speaker to talk about the products (first) and not the money. Again, I believe that the product is the key *to* the money. Then, get a few testimonials from the audience (give each person 3-minutes max).

Then, give them a break, but not before telling them that this next session will be about the business and the money. If they did their "job right" on the product, and had good testimonials, those who are interested will stay.

Those who were "tricked" into thinking this was a party and not an opportunity meeting about a home-based business can go home. Ones who are not interested can do the name; neither is an asset.

If you have products to show, put them on a table to the side and covered. If you put them on the table behind you, everyone will look at the products wondering *"what is the person trying to sell me"* and will not pay attention to what you are saying.

Then, UNCOVER the products from a table on the side or at the rear of the room like the unveiling of a statue. If you have a film, show them the film. There's no reason to "pressure them" into anything; they won't stay with the business. Make it a PRODUCTION! Make it FUN!

The exception is, of course, if you have a product to demonstrate. Even then, use only the product that you use for the demonstration. I do not recommend that you "line up" products in formation like soldiers; it confuses people.

Yes, go to a meeting *before* you drag a prospect to one. If you like the presenter, bring people to that meeting. If not, find a meeting that you enjoy, and bring your prospect to it. A bad meeting will cause you to lose a prospect you might have "worked on" for weeks or months.

Oh! Do not come to a meeting alone; bring someone *with* you? Always bring at least one guest. Try to bring several. For a "numbers game" to work, you have to bring *numbers* to the meeting. Hard work alone doesn't "cut it," add smart work and it will be difficult to fail.

The product is foremost, but the end result is trying to get others to "work the business." That's how you get rich. Get others working for you, duplicate yourself and earn *residual* income.

GETTING THEM TO A MEETING

In all Network Marketing companies you are asked to make a list of friends, neighbors, and relatives when you first get involved in this business. Actually, make a list of EVERYONE YOU KNOW; it's smart business. But how you approach them makes a difference. Get them *to* a meeting.

This is one of the most difficult things to do in this business. Here's some good pointers on that. TELL THEM THE TRUTH! Talk to them. Tell them you are involved (or thinking of getting involved) with a new company, and that you want them to tell you what they think, that you'd like their help.

Tell them (friend, neighbor, relative, acquaintance) , that you respect their opinion, and that you'd like their advice. *Everyone* has an opinion, and who doesn't like giving advice?

Most people are nice and will help. You read about, and hear about, and see on TV all the "bad" people in the world, whereas most are good people and only the tragic news and the "rotten apples" make news. Sad, but true.

If it's someone you recently met, they will be flattered that you asked *their* advice, *their* opinion and *their* help. Yes, (*almost*) everyone loves to help.

I have listened to hundreds talk about how to get someone to a meeting. At one training session, one person said, "*The way to get someone to a meeting,*

Mr. Billac, is to GO TO THEIR HOME AND PICK THEM UP! That way," he advised, "*you are certain they will be there.*" I laughed.

SOMETIMES, a "dream stealer" intervenes and tells them that it's a Pyramid Scheme. This *could* cause even your best friend to change their mind.

I've known instances where the person to be picked up (who has been approached by a *dream stealer*) locks their doors, turns out all the lights, and gets the entire family to lie down on the floor and hold their breath. Then, when the "door knocker" or "bell ringer" tires and leaves, they'll *lie to them* the next day.

If they agree to help you with their advice by attending a meeting, and if they live close or are on the way, why not pick them up?

BUT, agree on "about" the time that you plan to get there, and when you arrive and step out of your car, bend over a bit, smile and **wave at the house!**

Make it a fun game. IF the one you're to pick up is there, and they see you *wave* at the house and they are peeping through their curtains or blinds, they will think that you *saw* them and they will answer the door!

Dumb, you think? Stupid, you think? Won't work, you think? Wrong, WRONG, and **WRONG!** It is a bit silly, but it works. Have fun in this business; play it like a game.

Chapter 5

MONEY

Let's talk about **MONEY**. Money has one sense; **hearing.** If you tell it "*right,*" it will make you *more* money. If you tell it "*wrong,*" you LOSE money. And if you let it just set, inflation will nibble away at it until it is *almost* all gone.

Do I think that YOU can make money in Network Marketing? **YES I DO!** Why? Because **ANYONE CAN DO IT!** Find the product, pay plan, company, get training, and LEARN. I can honestly tell you that **THE SKY'S THE LIMIT!**

I know (and know *of*) thousands of people who are making a quarter of a million dollars a year in Network Marketing who have worked for as little as a year or two. Match THAT with a college degree—in almost anything?

I'm not "knocking" college, but graduating from college doesn't insure financial success. It does, however, give you "*more chips when you go up to the table to roll the dice.*" An EDUCATION is certainly important, but what you do WITH that knowledge is how you become FINANCIALLY successful.

I meet *new millionaires* at EVERY convention I attend. I have testimonials from several, SOME who

FAILED at a few other Network Marketing companies before finding "the one" that was "right" for them.

SOME SUCCESS STORIES

I know a 26-year-old former pizza delivery boy (from West Virginia) without a high school education who— within ONE year—was earning **$40,000 a month** in Network Marketing! I SAW HIS CHECKS!

In Houston, about 10 years ago, I met an 83-year-old *blind lady* who was earning $7,000 a month after eight months in her Network Marketing company. I SAW *HER* CHECKS!

And a young man, 37 years old, SAVED his parents' ranch in Canada by getting involved in an *Internet* Marketing company. The ranch had been in the family for four generations and it was about to go into foreclosure. But the son, in eight months, was earning $50,000 a WEEK! That's right, **$50,000 a WEEK**. I saw **HIS** checks, too!

Another person I wrote about in one of my books (I call him "the alien" now lives in a million-dollar beachfront home in Australia) made millions in Network Marketing. In every one of these companies, there are one or two whom, for WHATEVER reason, make more money than they can count.

"*The alien*" earned a bit over **TWO million dollars** his first year, and **SEVEN million** the following year. He worked hard and smart. He put in 16 to 18 hours a day, seven days a week for only SIX MON-THS, and he made a fortune. IF you find a company with the right product, good management, good training, and you work it hard and smart, you have a CHANCE to do it too. I can never PROMISE or GUARANTEE anything, just TELL you about it. The rest is up to you.

THE MILLIONAIRES

I feel it's time to put *names,* and even pictures WITH the names, to these people who have made BIG money in Network Marketing. I won't put any telephone numbers or addresses for security reasons. I have "written permission" from the following.

A MILLION DOLLAR BONUS

WHO, for instance, earns a MILLION DOLLAR **BONUS?** Rick and Brenda Ricketts have, Ron and Judy Head have, and P.J. (Pete) Jensen has.

Ron and Judy Head

Rick and Brenda Ricketts

P.J. (Pete) Jenson

Juliet St. John

Juliet has earned over a million dollars, and "her" bonus is coming up soon.

I don't want to scare you with that *"million-dollar"* talk. The following have earned only a *half* million in this exciting new company.

Bill and Anne Hoffman
Jerome Hughes
Katrina Greenhill
Dave and Marliss Funk
Floyd and Carla Williams
James and Marcia Prewitt
Steve Branch
T.V. Wilson
Arlyne Thompson

What I'd like you to understand, please, is that many of these people are "ordinary" individuals who found the right product, the right company and they *went after* their dream; each is living that dream!

This company that they are working for *guarantees* you a minimum of $500 per month. Also, once you reach a certain (very attainable) level, you are *guaranteed* $24,000 a year just to hold *one meeting per month!* Whatever else you earn is *gravy*. What other company does this?

I was at a meeting with about 300 positive, enthusiastic, *caring* people. Corporate had TRIPLED the Christmas Bonus of their 129 employees, and several of the leaders *added* a hundred or so thousand dollars *more* to thank them for helping them with their business. Yes, one big family. I had never seen anything quite like this before.

This company that wants and helps their associates to make money. They have a *BILL OF RIGHTS* that states the company has *insured* the funds their associates have earned. They also will not make changes in their pay plan. It's sure "death" to companies that do.

CAN I REALLY DO IT?

YES you can! ANYBODY can do it if they WANT to. Make Network Marketing fun. I've met new friends that I truly care for. These folks, especially the ones who are successful, **DO** have more fun than most others. They meet at conventions, go to nice dinners, meet in Hawaii, Paris, Rome, ski resorts—SOME even come visit me here in Texas.

And, it **IS** possible for YOU, no matter **who or where you are,** to do these things if you CHOOSE. First, you must HAVE desire, ACT on that desire, get focused, and work smart. Yes, *"If you think you can, or think you can't, you're right."* When I say **ANYONE CAN DO IT,** it is **FACT!**

I've seen 26 -year-old "kids" earning $35,000 **a MONTH**. My father-in-law, an engineer with THREE degrees, STILL does not believe it. He SEES it when he travels with me but still DOES NOT BELIEVE IT!

Remember, those who do NOT believe, and if THIS BOOK doesn't *cause* them **to** believe, **NOTHING will change their minds!** Don't WASTE time on anyone who does not "see" as you do. **SW, SW, SW, N. Some WILL, some WON'T, so WHAT, NEXT.**

Smile, pass them up, pray for them and go make a LOT of money. And MONEY is the reason to do this. If you HELP people **and** earn money doing it, your heart is in the "right place" and you WILL succeed!

"MONEY doesn't buy HAPPINESS,
but it certainly makes MISERY easy to endure."

Chapter 6

PRODUCTS SPELL SUCCESS

THE RIGHT PRODUCT

If I mention finding the RIGHT PRODUCT a **few DOZEN TIMES** in this book, it's not *Alzheimer's*, it's FACT! Without a doubt, the **FIRST THING** you should look for is a company with a *UNIQUE* **PRODUCT or SERVICE.**

      With a PRODUCT, absolutely NEVER sell; **USE AND RECOMMEND!** Do your customer a FAVOR and tell them about what you're marketing, what you BELIEVE in and FIND something that almost everyone NEEDS (or wants), that is CHEAPER and/or can be delivered *faster* than a competitive product. For you to become successful (remember) that product or service **must** appeal to the MASSES and cause them to:

        ☆ **Feel better**
        ☆ **Look better**
        ☆ **Live longer**
        ☆ **Get things done quicker**
        ☆ **Enjoy life more**
        ☆ **Save them money**
        ☆ **Make them money**
        ☆ **Cut their utility bills**

THE PRODUCT IS VITAL! Think about it. If the product is the same as *everyone else has*, what are your odds? Think of any number of products—ones that work—that are safe and fun that *you* would be inclined to buy.

YOU CHOOSE THE PRODUCT

I promised you, at the beginning of this book, that I would give you products that I researched and that I feel would be some of which you might choose to go into business for yourself.

My friends, investigating these companies and the people behind them is my business, and I am good at it. I spend tens of thousand of dollars and months (or more) of research *before* I decide to write about any of these businesses.

I use top-notch attorneys, experienced MLM experts and my personal "visits" at companies—many who have no idea who I am or what I'm doing there—I don't sell their products. Nor do I work for them. This research is to help YOU!

I *never* list company names, but I tell you the products that appeal to the masses; products people want, need, or should have. Next are the "products" that I and my team of experts agree upon, and I wanted to tell you about *some* of what to look for. I want you to succeed. The more you do succeed, the more books I sell.

THE TRAVEL BUSINESS

See if this "product" makes sense to you. TRAVEL is a SEVEN TRILLION DOLLAR A YEAR INDUSTRY. It's said that this figure will double in the next several years. *Somebody* is making a commission on this, why not you? Everybody travels.

There's a new "baby boomer" reaching 60 years of age every EIGHT SECONDS for the next 20 years. Most of the "boomers" made good money and the thing they want to do most when they retire is TRAVEL.

Because of the computer, and being able to get fast service and the best prices by using the Internet, in the past several years more than 200,000 travel agents are no longer working this business.

This company (the one that paid those four people a MILLION DOLLAR BONUS) has a search engine where with the punch of a few keys you can book your flights, cruises, vacation packages, hotel and rental cars at competitive prices.

Their growth is outstanding, they have never failed paying a check or a bill in the past five years (since they started this business) and all you need to do is *tell* your friends, relatives and neighbors about this, guide them to your web site.

It truly is easy; you tell, they punch a few keys and the computer will do the rest. You simply *guide* others and wait for your check. You will save *them* money, *you save* money and you *make* money. Why wouldn't those you tell take this route?

I took a lot of time in this investigation. I met those "behind" this company. I have never seen anything like it. The corporate officers have integrity, they have successful business experience, and they have money. They have been in business almost 6 years and their growth is unbelievable. They are at the beginning of a *trend* that is skyrocketing.

It costs little to "be in business for yourself" and you get all the help imaginable. I truly like these people and I like the business. Take a few minutes to find out more about them. You will be awestruck!

INDOOR AIR PURIFIERS

Maybe 3% of people in all of North America have them; almost everyone *needs* them! This is a product to market that is unique and needed. People just don't know about it. Let's talk about WHY?

Since the Arab Oil Embargo in the early 1980s, we were told by our government to conserve energy; to keep the warm air inside during the winter and the cool air inside during the summer. To do this we had to "close our homes" to the outside world.

Great idea, right? Well, it was a "money-*saving* idea" but we literally *bulletproofed* our homes where they couldn't breathe. There are dust mites, viruses, mold and mildew that are literally "locked" inside your home and people are getting sick and don't know why.

I discovered that INDOOR AIR POLLUTION can be 5-10 times WORSE than the outside stuff, and is a major cause of many illnesses. An INDOOR AIR PURIFIER is necessary. The thing is, you have to be academic and choose the right one.

Young children and the elderly are effected most by this INDOOR *polluted* air. The immune system in the young isn't fully developed, and with the elderly, their immune system has weakened. Even those in the middle are affected because this is *cumulative*.

The *American College of Allergists* state: "*HALF of all illnesses are caused by polluted INDOOR air.*" The EPA says: "*INDOOR air pollution is America's most serious environmental problem affecting the health of humans.*"The problem is that very FEW even *know* about this. I didn't. When people spoke of "polluted air" I just assumed them meant the OUTSIDE stuff.

There is a company that provides you with these machines that produces *INSIDE air* that smells like the outside air after a thunderstorm; clean, fresh and healthy. It's used to rid the smell of a wet basement, it takes the SMOKE SMELL out of cars. It's wondrous.

They also market the best water purifying machines on the market. AND, their prices are the BEST I've been able to find. I've visited manufacturing facilities all over the world: Europe, Southeast Asia and the United States. And, I found that great combination, "the BEST and the LEAST EXPENSIVE."

There are many of these "machines" on the market. You need to look on your computer and COMPARE. If you want to help others and help yourself, hit www.naturalairproducts.com and learn more. This is yet another great product to start a home-based business.

Look for a combination *ionizer* and *ozoneator*. So very many people suffer from migraine headaches, sinus problems, feel tired all the time, watery eyes and mood swings. Also, many illnesses are worsened by INDOOR polluted air. This is a terrific PRODUCT and you can TRY it before you buy it.

VITAMIN SUPPLEMENTS

Of the TOP 30 home-based business companies in the WORLD, vitamins hold 20 or more of the 30 spots. The reason WHY is because HEALTH is so vital to a happy existence and surely everyone wants to FEEL good.

EVERYONE has a "*secret pill*" or "*miracle potion*" whereas few of these, if any, exists. Our body is a miraculous machine, but to KEEP this machine "*oiled and lubricated*" takes serious thought. We'd ALL be poor if we bought EVERY vitamin we're told by experts to try or that we see advertised on TV. Let's talk sense:

The SOIL has been "nutrient depleted" for more than fifty years. If you'd like to get all the *essential* vitamins and minerals you need, EXPERTS tell me you'd have to eat about **65 POUNDS** of food each day.

A truly TERRIFIC product on the market is called SABA (*Swahilli* for SEVEN). This product is an adaptogen FORMULA that is probably *the* most proven product in history. There's a good story behind it.

Russians wanted to be world dominant with their military, their Cosmonauts and their Olympic athletes. A team of more than 1,400 Red Chinese and Russian scientist were sent to the *Primorye* section of Russia to study plants and fruit to find a true "miracle potion."

It took them FORTY years to come up with a product (SABA) that helps you "manage" stress. Dr. Israel Brekhman spearheaded this research and tested it on factory workers, athletes, the military and the *Bolshoi* ballet. The results were phenomenal. When the Iron Curtain "went down" Dr. Brekhman shared his findings with the world and now WE have it.

"Others" *claim to* have adaptogens, but it's Dr. Brekhman's adaptogen *formula* with those seven ingredients that is the very best. Not only THAT but "our" scientists were able to add POMEGRANATE to it. It truly DOES help manage stress, and it's now also "heart healthy" and it tastes GREAT!

Getting OLD is far better than the alternative (dying), but we want to get old PAIN FREE and retain our QUALITY of life. So, eat right and exercise. But what ABOUT vitamins? Which *do* we need?

My family and I have been taking Dr. Brekhman's adaptogenic formula for almost ten years.

BEFORE this I was gulping down 17 vitamin pills per day. Now I drink an ounce per day of SABA and NO pills. NONE OF us have had serious illness, just an occasional virus the kids "catch" at school.

The company that markets this formula can be found by emailing the person who gave or sent you this book. It is worth looking into. I back this product, business and corporate officers 100%. YOU make the choice. I'LL help train you.

The company CEO is a retired *Major GENERAL* with a PH.D. in marketing and with a highly successful career spearheading several other businesses.

They have the product, the business experience, and a competitive marketing plan and some terrific training tools. I was very impressed.

HEALTHY COFFEE

THIS is a sleeper. MORE THAN 1.4 BILLON cups of coffee are consumed daily throughout the world. (WHO counts that, I wondered?) This certainly is a CONSUMABLE. MOST people drink coffee or know others who do. THIS coffee is also HEALTHY because of the *Reishi* mushroom that gives it 185 antioxidants and has NO (almost none) caffeine.

Not only THAT, it is about one FOURTH the price of *Starbucks* that you buy in super markets. Had I been drinking this coffee for the past five years, I'd have 15 YEARS of FREE coffee.

It is extremely easy to "tell" about. You can tell others about it and they can order it—DELIVERED—without joining anything. If you want to work it as a business, the product is profound. If you want to invite others to join your "team" it's inexpensive and easy. The product is old, but *this* coffee is unique.

Also, everybody (almost everybody) drinks coffee. *This* coffee is healthy, there are several blends from which to choose, and it is less expensive. What a great product to *tell* others about. It's worth "looking into" even if you only want to buy the coffee.

LEGAL INSURANCE

People have HEALTH, LIFE, HOMEOWNERS, AUTO-MOBILE and BOAT insurance—even insurance on their dog and cat, but NOT insurance against being *sued.* Yet, your chance of being sued is *three times* that of your being admitted into a hospital. And the price it costs to get a competent attorney is extremely *steep*.

This is the "era of litigation;" everyone is suing or *being* sued for just about everything. Those who are not wealthy always seem to get *"the short end of the stick,"* but not anymore.

If you have legal insurance you can retain one of the best law firms in your state for LESS THAN **one-dollar a day**. Is it worth it? I say yes! And I, personally, saved thousands of dollars the first two years that I bought this insurance.

You can help so many "nice" folks who can't afford a high-priced attorney, and make a very good living while doing it. This is a product that just about everyone needs. To buy (and sell) *legal* insurance is featured in a book I wrote, appropriately titled . . . *JUSTICE IS GREEN.*

I don't understand why every person selling insurance person doesn't include it when they talk about life, health, automobile or any kind of insurance. It is a professional home-based business, and the company has an excellent pay plan, with highly competent leadership and training.

In addition, they are featuring an *Identity Theft Protection* plan; ask them about it! It is inexpensive and small businesses need it.

I am listing some of the PRODUCTS I researched to give you an "idea" of some of what is "out there." You must choose what appeals to you the most. Check it out using the criteria that I feel you should follow, and have fun making money.

FINAL INFO

I have met with hundreds of people from around the WORLD; cab drivers, airline pilots, real estate salespersons, store clerks, secretaries, housewives, carpenters, ministers, garbage collectors, policemen, (that *pizza* delivery boy), and almost any and every job and profession you can imagine. All became from well-off to wealthy in Network Marketing.

Whatever reason you can think of NOT to try Network Marketing, I could give you tens of thousands of reasons TO try. I have dozens of Network Marketers who visit me each year here at my ranch in Texas. And I am invited to visit them at their *villa* in Spain, at their ranch in Brazil at their ski lodge in Aspen and at vacation spots around the world.

These people are living *"the good life,"* and do you know what? They were ALL working at JOBS before this. Most are no longer working—at all. And THAT is what I want for you. You just have to make up your mind to TRY.

Don't you feel that you could truly succeed in this business if you find all the "ingredients" I tell you to look for in a company? Isn't it worth a modest investment and some TIME to find out if this is for you? You know my answer; I say **GO FOR IT!**

Everything in life is made up of choices. Born poor? So WHAT? Choose never to be poor again. How about a home-based business? It's up to *you* to choose. Yes, throughout life you have choices.

I'm not a *rah-rah* type of guy, but I'm passionate about whatever I do. If you *do* make a choice, go after it with a passion. There is never need to exaggerate or lie about a product or the money that you or any other person makes. If you make the right choice, and if you find the product, pay plan, leadership etc., you can tell the truth. And if you work hard and smart, you have a CHANCE to make a LOT of money.

CONTACT the person who gave you this book. Find out if THEIR product is one that you like, get information from them, investigate yourself and MAKE IT HAPPEN! It is "up to you."

Donald Trump IS one of the richest men in the world. Know what he says it takes to be successful?

"First," he says, *"you must LIKE what you're doing. Next, you must LEARN what you're talking about."* These, however, are but the first TWO ingredients. But, added to this you must then have **DESIRE** and **FOCUS**. With Network Marketing you must also LIKE people (or PRETEND that you do).

I'VE GOT A DEAL FOR *YOU*

At least *three times* a week I am called, faxed, or e-mailed about some new *"business opportunity"* or *"a deal"* that will make me rich. When people call up with such enthusiasm about their new product and/or company, and tell me how terrific it is, I listen.

Of *course* it's the best—it's *their* chosen company—and chances are that with *this* enthusiasm and belief, they'll *make* it work. This doesn't mean, however, that this *company* or their product IS good.

The first thing I need to know is WHY is THEIR product the best? Exactly how much *research* has this excited caller done on this product? WHO is going to buy this product? What MAKES it better than the others, and/or WHY is it unique?

Chances are they know NONE of these answers. They attended a meeting and "heard" what the person in the front of the room *told* them. They liked what they heard, they might have been anxious to make more money, and they liked the product.

This isn't enough, my friends. YOU have to do research. My advice is not to be rushed into ANY-THING; there is always TIME. It takes time to check this out, and it takes time to do the necessary "home-work" I've told you about.

ALL Network Marketers (or is it *Marketeers?*) are taught to counter objections, and one of the main objections from those you are trying to interest in your business is *"Let me think about it."*

These Network Marketing *persons* want you to act NOW. So, instead of saying you want to *think* about it, tell them you'd like some time to do some checking.

Tell them what you'd like to know and have THEM get these answers for you. Then, once you get those answers and feel "comfortable" with the answers (and if the PRODUCT is one you like and that "the masses" want or need) there is NO NEED to "think about it" further: **GO FOR IT!**

My part in all of this is to help both those who are in a company and trying to interest someone to join, and for those of you who are looking for a part-time, home-based business TO join.

Network Marketing IS the answer. When you find the right product, it all starts there. Then do your checking, ask questions about the pay plan, company and the training. A good *sponsor* is important also. Ask THEM how they are going to help you.

Just for safety, get the names and information of the ones who sponsored *them*—and the one above that person—in the event something "happens" to your immediate sponsor. It is a wonderful business.

Choose a product and follow the guidelines I tell you about in this book. Once you have done your "homework," get busy and change your financial life FOREVER. Truthfully, You *can* do it. Or rather, *you* can do it. Either way, please, don't sit and hope for success, go after it.

And remember . .

"If you think you can, or think you CAN'T,
YOU'RE RIGHT!"

AUTHOR'S CLOSING COMMENTS

It depends on what **YOU** do, on the choice **YOU** make, and THIS BOOK tells you HOW to do it. It gives you CHOICES. And yes, the rest is up to **YOU.**

NEVER allow a *DREAM STEALER* to cause you to NOT try; a few years working a successful Network Marketing business very well **could** make you financially solvent for the **REST OF YOUR LIFE!**

Do NOT get discouraged if EVERYONE doesn't listen to what you have to say or become interested in what you are doing. LEARN this business and this makes you confident, and DO play it like a game.

Some people get discouraged because it doesn't happen fast enough; it will NOT happen overnight. But it's the fastest, easiest, *least expensive* method I know of to start your own business. Have FUN doing it and play it like a GAME. In TIME it usually happens; TIME is your ally.

LEADS truly are one of THE most important parts of this business. If you join a business and run out of leads and need my help, I have a program that is **FREE** and my NEWSLETTER is also FREE.

My "chosen mission" is to HELP those who want to make a success of their life. F o r m y **F R E E Information Packet**, e-mail me.

Yes, contact me anytime. That's why I say— again and again . . .

ANYONE CAN DO IT!

ABOUT THE AUTHOR

PETE BILLAC is one of the most sought-after speakers in the USA and in many other parts of the world. He has written 58 books; 47 have sold over million copies each. His worldwide best seller, HOW NOT TO BE LONELY, sold more than seven MILLION copies.

His books are published in 14 languages.

Pete is a maverick; he writes what pleases him. He is a *"tell it like it is"* kind of guy whose topics range from adventure and war to the Mafia, relationships, famous people, health, motivation and business.

He speaks to Fortune 500 companies on marketing, and he lectures at conventions and at universities across the globe. He delivers his "messages" with a mixture of common sense and knowledge. He charms his audiences with his winning smile, quick wit and candor; he breathes life into every topic. He makes his audiences laugh—hard! For fun, he conducts lectures on cruise ships.

"This book tells people how to realize their potential and get out of their financial quagmire. Making money is not difficult if you believe in yourself and work smart. God wants you to be prosperous, and to help others."

Perhaps you've seen Pete on Donahue, Sally Jessy Raphael, Good Morning America, Laff Stop and/or other national television shows.

"Pete is an expert at restoring self-confidence and self-esteem in others . . ."

Phil Donahue
National Television Talk Show Host

YOUR HOME-BASED BUSINESS

AND

HOW TO MAKE IT WORK

Swan Publishing
Southwind Ranch
1059 CR 100
Burnet, TX 78611

(512) 756-6800
Fax   (512) 756-0102

Visit our web site at: swan-pub.com
E-mail: pete@swan-pub.com

FOR MORE INFORMATION:

After reading this book, please pass it on to a friend or relative. It could change their financial lives forever!